Growth in the Garden

66 Notes on Self-Growth and Self-Development

To my gardeners:

Thank you for planting seeds and tending to them as they mature and blossom

Growth in the Garden

Living life in the fast lane picking up and moving with each transition of life...from high school to college; from college to graduate school; from graduate school to a new city; and living in three different places within the first year of being in a new city, it was hard to not feel like I was running from something, if not everything, and neglecting myself. Growth in the Garden takes you on my journey of how I made it a habit to focus and commit to slowing down and spending time with myself to dig myself out of the dark moments of my past in order to thrive in the moment. I was able to discover who I am versus what I do, my purpose and how to live in it, and get to the root of lingering issues. I hope your journey is as rewarding as mine.

Taneka Lewis

In a study published in the *European Journal of Social Psychology* it takes, on average, 66 days for a new habit to form; so I challenge you to commit to 66 days of daily reading and putting these notes into practice. Take 5 to 10 minutes out of your day to either read, meditate, pray, and/or reflect on each note. Whether it is in the morning before your day gets started to help set your intentions for the day, in the middle of the day on your lunch break to help you shift your mindset throughout the day, at night before you close your eyes to go to sleep to help you reflect on your day, or all three. This will help you to take a deeper look at yourself and evaluate how you are navigating your journey.

With each note recall a personal situation that relates to the note. Ask yourself where you went wrong and how can this note help you to not make the same mistakes again. It may be uncomfortable but often times we have to put ourselves in those situations to grow.

Welcome to Growth in the Garden.

Growth (noun): the progressive development physically, mentally, emotionally, or spiritually

Garden (noun): a well-cultivated region that is symbolic of self

Post your favorite notes and Bible verses on social media and tag me @type_tee

Affirmation #1

On this journey, I will commit to the art of consistency and obsession of tending to my garden and maximizing my personal growth and development. I will explore and evaluate the things I have manifested to live out my destiny.

Place your name in the affirmation (i.e. I, (insert name) will...) and for the next 33 days read this three times at least twice a day; once silently to yourself, once out loud, and once out loud while looking at yourself in the mirror.

Taneka Lewis

Note #1

In order to grow you must first be planted because you cannot address something that is not revealed. Bury who you thought you were and allow your true self to show.

"Be diligent in these matters; give yourself wholly to them, so that everyone may see your progress."

1 Timothy 4:15, NIV

Note #1 Reflections

Taneka Lewis

Note #2

Everything is not going to provide you nourishment. Be careful who you trust, even dirt looks like soil.

All my enemies whisper together against me; they imagine the worst for me, saying, "A vile disease has afflicted him; he will never get up from the place where he lies." Even my close friend, someone I trusted, one who shared my bread, has turned against me.

Psalm 41:7-9, NIV

Note #2 Reflections

Taneka Lewis

Note #3

Nobody can take anything that is meant for you so claim what is yours and go get it!

And we know that God causes everything to work together for the good of those who love God and are called according to his purpose for them.

Romans 8:28, NIV

Note #3 Reflections

Note #4

Anything aspiring growth and development is worth the struggle.

I consider that our present sufferings are not worth comparing with the glory that will be revealed in us.

Romans 8:18, NIV

Note #4 Reflections

Taneka Lewis

Note #5

You possess the power to change yourself, not the power to change someone else.

Have I any help in me, when resource is driven from me?

Job 6:13, ESV

Note #5 Reflections

Taneka Lewis

Note #6

Everything you have is not for everybody so do not fault them for not understanding your journey.

In their hearts humans plan their course, but the LORD establishes their steps.

Proverbs 16:9, NIV

Note #6 Reflections

Taneka Lewis

Note #7

Everybody wants to "make it out" but acknowledge where you are and make it count, prepare yourself doing all the little things to be ready to seize your opportunity.

Let us not become weary in doing good, for at the proper time we will reap a harvest if we do not give up.

Galatians 6:9, NIV

Note #7 Reflections

Note #8

No one ever enters a war with the intent to lose but one side is always wrong so if it hinders your growth, uproot it and plant something new.

But he said, "Don't delay me. The LORD has made my mission successful; now send me back so I can return to my master."

Genesis 24:56, NLT

Note #8 Reflections

Taneka Lewis

Note #9

Seeds do not grow unless they are watered. People may have counted you out and doubted you; but in essence they watered what was already planted to spark your growth.

Count it all joy, my brothers, when you meet trials of various kinds, for you know that the testing of your faith produces steadfastness. And let steadfastness have its full effect, that you may be perfect and complete, lacking in nothing.

James 1:2-4, ESV

Note #9 Reflections

Taneka Lewis

Note #10

Detach from the things that drain, distract, and destroy you. You control what deserves your time, attention, and energy. Walk away from the negative things that do not help you grow.

Be wise in the way you act toward outsiders; make the most of every opportunity.

Colossians 4:5, NIV

Growth in the Garden

Note #10 Reflections

Taneka Lewis

Note #11

You plan everything else except time to spend with yourself. Self-care is important; you need time alone to be a better you. Always be mindful of yourself.

Those who are kind benefit themselves, but the cruel bring ruin on themselves.

Proverbs 11:17, NIV

Note #11 Reflections

What does self-care look like for you?
How can you prioritize time to spend with yourself?

_____
_____
_____
_____
_____
_____
_____
_____
_____
_____
_____
_____
_____
_____
_____
_____
_____
_____
_____
_____

Taneka Lewis

Note #12

You do not always have to be strong. A moment of weakness does not define your strength. So cry; water your garden, because everything meant to destroy you gives you a chance to grow stronger. Let it all out!

But he said to me, "My grace is sufficient for you, for my power is made perfect in weakness." Therefore I will boast all the more gladly about my weaknesses, so that Christ's power may rest on me.

2 Corinthians 12:9, NIV

Growth in the Garden

Note #12 Reflections

Taneka Lewis

Note #13

Strength and endurance is not about how much you can handle and how long you can last before you break; it is about how much you can handle and how long you can last after you break. Catch your second wind, you are just getting started.

but those who hope in the LORD will renew their strength. They will soar on wings like eagles; they will run and not grow weary, they will walk and not be faint.

Isaiah 40:31, NIV

Note #13 Reflections

Taneka Lewis

Note #14

Do not let other people's limitations define you to be something you do not want to be; create your own "titles" of who you want to be and take ownership of it. Become more of yourself every day.

Obviously, I'm not trying to win the approval of people, but of God. If pleasing people were my goal, I would not be Christ's servant.

Galatians 1:10, NLT

Note #14 Reflections

Taneka Lewis

Note #15

Do not let pride be the source of your pain. You are human and it is ok to need and ask for help. Put people in your circle that have your best interest at heart.

Where there is strife, there is pride, but wisdom is found in those who take advice.

Proverbs 13:10, NIV

Note #15 Reflections

Taneka Lewis

Note #16

Excellence is the desire for continuous progression. Perfection lies within your persistence to seek and live out excellence. Today be greater than you have ever been.

Your righteousness, O God, reaches to the highest heavens. You have done such wonderful things. Who can compare with you, O God? You have allowed me to suffer much hardship, but you will restore me to life again and lift me up from the depths of the earth. You will restore me to even greater honor and comfort me once again.

Psalm 71:19-21, NLT

Growth in the Garden

Note #16 Reflections

Taneka Lewis

Note #17

Break the unhealthy patterns of your past. Do not recycle experiences that can sabotage your potential growth. Old habits do not take you to new heights. Allow yourself the opportunity to ultimately achieve all that you desire.

Be very careful, then, how you live—not as unwise but as wise, making the most of every opportunity, because the days are evil.

Ephesians 5:15-16, NIV

Note #17 Reflections

Taneka Lewis

Note #18

Fear suffocates the imagination. Do not let self-doubt dismantle your dreams. Believe in and trust your vision. Sometimes you will be the only one that can see it. Take a leap into the unknown and encounter new experiences, take that risk.

Don't worry about anything; instead, pray about everything. Tell God what you need, and thank him for all he has done. Then you will experience God's peace, which exceeds anything we can understand. His peace will guard your hearts and minds as you live in Christ Jesus.

Philippians 4:6-7, NLT

Note #18 Reflections

Taneka Lewis

Note #19

Your ultimate freedom lies within your ability to decide how the things outside of you affect you. Look within for the things cannot provided by others.

"I have the right to do anything," you say—but not everything is beneficial. "I have the right to do anything"—but I will not be mastered by anything.

1 Corinthians 6:12, NIV

Note #19 Reflections

Taneka Lewis

Note #20

Begin to question and challenge yourself because you often discover what you will do by finding out what you will not do.

Call to me and I will answer you, and will tell you great and hidden things that you have not known.

Jeremiah 33:3, ESV

Note #20 Reflections

Taneka Lewis

Note #21

Cultivate silence and stillness in your life. Take a break from all distractions and just be. Enjoy your existence and protect your peace.

a time to tear and a time to mend, a time to be silent and a time to speak,

Ecclesiastes 3:7, NIV

Growth in the Garden

Note #21 Reflections

Taneka Lewis

Note #22

A seed planted in cement will not bloom into a beautiful flower. Be mindful of where you plant your seeds and what you feed your environment; it will make or break your growth.

And now, just as you accepted Christ Jesus as your Lord, you must continue to follow him. Let your roots grow down into him, and let your lives be built on him. Then your faith will grow strong in the truth you were taught, and you will overflow with thankfulness.

Colossians 2:6-7, NLT

Note #22 Reflections

In what ways can you improve your surroundings and be more aware of the environment you are putting yourself in? Acknowledge the different people you're around, things you watch, and listen to; make note of how they affect you both positively and negatively and make the necessary changes for you to thrive.

_____
_____
_____
_____
_____
_____
_____
_____
_____
_____
_____
_____
_____
_____
_____
_____
_____
_____
_____
_____

Taneka Lewis

Note #23

Love yourself in a way that deflects indifference. Get rid of the clouds trying to block your sunshine, inhibiting your seeds from growing; this inhibits the growth in your garden.

Above all, clothe yourselves with love, which binds us all together in perfect harmony.

Colossians 3:14, NLT

Note #23 Reflections

Taneka Lewis

Note #24

Be transparent with yourself and your journey so you can acknowledge and appreciate all that you are worth.

Nothing in all creation is hidden from God. Everything is naked and exposed before his eyes, and he is the one to whom we are accountable.

Hebrews 4:13, NLT

Note #24 Reflections

Taneka Lewis

Note #25

Focus on where you are going and not on what you have been through or are going through. Do not delay or hinder your forward progression because of something behind you.

"Forget the former things; do not dwell on the past. See, I am doing a new thing! Now it springs up; do you not perceive it? I am making a way in the wilderness and streams in the wasteland.

Isaiah 43:18-19, NIV

Note #25 Reflections

Taneka Lewis

Note #26

You will not discover what you are capable of unless you try; take a chance on yourself. Change will not come without a challenge so find comfort in your growing pains.

I planted the seed, Apollos watered it, but God has been making it grow. So neither the one who plants nor the one who waters is anything, but only God, who makes things grow. The one who plants and the one who waters have one purpose, and they will each be rewarded according to their own labor.

1 Corinthians 3:6-8, NIV

Note #26 Reflections

Taneka Lewis

Note #27

Delayed does not mean denied. Do not confuse diligence with defeat. Great things take time and effort. Be patient. It is not always about the speed but the direction.

Then the Lord said to me, "Write my answer plainly on tablets, so that a runner can carry the correct message to others. This vision is for a future time. It describes the end, and it will be fulfilled. If it seems slow in coming, wait patiently, for it will surely take place. It will not be delayed.

Habakkuk 2:2-3, NLT

Growth in the Garden

Note #27 Reflections

Taneka Lewis

Note #28

Issues only become problems when you refuse to accept you have them or when you refuse to acknowledge that you are imperfect. Address the issue.

We all stumble in many ways. Anyone who is never at fault in what they say is perfect, able to keep their whole body in check.

James 3:2, NIV

Growth in the Garden

Note #28 Reflections

Taneka Lewis

Note #29

Your experiences shape your expertise to guide your journey of evolution. Do not be a victim of your pain, use it to fuel your journey. Heal from it to create your platform for your growth.

Blessed is the one who perseveres under trial because, having stood the test, that person will receive the crown of life that the Lord has promised to those who love him.

James 1:12, NIV

Who comforts us in all our troubles, so that we can comfort those in any trouble with the comfort we ourselves receive from God.

2 Corinthians 1:4, NIV

Note #29 Reflections

Taneka Lewis

Note #30

Do not blame other people's actions for what you are going through. Some people are placed in your life to help you help yourself. Take responsibility to deal with your pain and trauma to free yourself.

Pay careful attention to your own work, for then you will get the satisfaction of a job well done, and you won't need to compare yourself to anyone else. For we are each responsible for our own conduct.

Galatians 6:4-5, NLT

Note #30 Reflections

Taneka Lewis

Note #31

Growth is painful. Change is painful. Change does not always equal growth. It is possible to change without growing; however, it is impossible to grow without changing. If you feel like you are in "hell" do not stop because nothing is as painful as staying stuck somewhere you do not belong.

For I am about to do something new. See, I have already begun! Do you not see it? I will make a pathway through the wilderness. I will create rivers in the dry wasteland.

Isaiah 43:19, NLT

Note #31 Reflections

Taneka Lewis

Note #32

As you explore the 'why behind your what', you will experience obstacles, like every journey, but you have to look outside of your obstacles to make it through them.

Therefore this is what the LORD says: "I will put obstacles before this people. Parents and children alike will stumble over them;...

Jeremiah 6:21, NIV

Note #32 Reflections

Taneka Lewis

Note #33

Have the wisdom to know the difference between what you want in your life versus what you need in your life and have the faith to seek it.

I pray that out of his glorious riches he may strengthen you with power through his Spirit in your inner being, so that Christ may dwell in your hearts through faith. And I pray that you, being rooted and established in love, may have power, together with all the Lord's holy people, to grasp how wide and long and high and deep is the love of Christ, and to know this love that surpasses knowledge—that you may be filled to the measure of all the fullness of God.

Ephesians 3: 16-19, NIV

Note #33 Reflections

What are six things that are a necessity in your life (things you cannot survive without)? What are six things you simply want in your life but can live without? How difficult is it for you to differentiate the two and why?

Taneka Lewis

Affirmation #1

On this journey, I will commit to the art of consistency and obsession of tending to my garden and maximizing my personal growth and development. I will explore and evaluate the things I have manifested to live out my destiny.

Place your name in the affirmation (i.e. I, (insert name) will...) and for the next 33 days read this three times at least twice a day; once silently to yourself, once out loud, and once out loud while looking at yourself in the mirror.

Affirmation #2

I will not be afraid to affirm the truth, my truth.
I will discover, decide, and define my distinction.
I will dismiss things that discourage my distinction.
I will devote my distinction to make a difference in my life and the world.

Place your name in the affirmation (i.e. I, (insert name) will...) and for the next 33 days read this three times at least twice a day; once silently to yourself, once out loud, and once out loud while looking at yourself in the mirror.

Note #34

Acknowledge and be aware of your thoughts. You are what you continuously think. Everything begins and ends in the mind. Thoughts become things.

Jesus knew what they were thinking, so he asked them, "Why do you have such evil thoughts in your hearts?

Matthew 9:4, NLT

Note #34 Reflections

Taneka Lewis

Note #35

In order to maximize your full potential you have to define and respect your boundaries. Saying *no* is not always a bad thing. Choose YOU!

> The day for building your walls will come,
> the day for extending your boundaries.
>
> Micah 7:11, NIV

Note #35 Reflections

Taneka Lewis

Note #36

Surrender to the journey of unpredictability and have the faith to step into the unknown when it comes to what is meant for you.

Trust in the LORD with all your heart and lean not on your own understanding;

Proverbs 3:5, NIV

Note #36 Reflections

Note #37

Movement does not always mean progression. Use other people's successes as motivation to progress in your life and not as a measuring stick to keep track of what you do and do not have.

But the fruit of the Spirit is love, joy, peace, forbearance, kindness, goodness, faithfulness, gentleness and self-control. Against such things there is no law. Those who belong to Christ Jesus have crucified the flesh with its passions and desires. Since we live by the Spirit, let us keep in step with the Spirit. Let us not become conceited, provoking and envying each other.

Galatians 5:22-26, NIV

Growth in the Garden

Note #37 Reflections

Note #38

Take a deep breath and slow down your thoughts. Give yourself the opportunity to create peace with your heart and mind.

And those who are peacemakers will plant seeds of peace and reap a harvest of righteousness.

James 3:18, NLT

Growth in the Garden

Note #38 Reflections

Taneka Lewis

Note #39

You are the only one that can figure out your comfort in dysfunction. You are the only one with your deeply rooted issues. Secure your insecurities. Do not run from your truth.

For the Spirit God gave us does not make us timid, but gives us power, love and self-discipline. So do not be ashamed of the testimony...

2 Timothy 1:7-8, NIV

Growth in the Garden

Note #39 Reflections

Taneka Lewis

Note #40

End the war between who you really are and who you pretend to be. Free yourself!

But the LORD said to Samuel, "Do not consider his appearance or his height, for I have rejected him. The LORD does not look at the things people look at. People look at the outward appearance, but the LORD looks at the heart."

1 Samuel 16:7, NIV

Growth in the Garden

Note #40 Reflections

Taneka Lewis

Note #41

Often times you are the culprit of your own downfall; being your greatest help and hurt. You allow yourself to believe excuses dressed up as "reasons." Stop tricking yourself!

Obviously, the law applies to those to whom it was given, for its purpose is to keep people from having excuses, ...

Romans 3:19, NLT

Note #41 Reflections

Note #42

Endure the pain of discipline or suffer through the pain of disappointment. The choice is yours.

Whoever heeds discipline shows the way to life, but whoever ignores correction leads others astray.

Proverbs 10:17, NIV

Note #42 Reflections

Note #43

There is great reward on the other side of fear so do not run away from that which you fear; it only increases the distance from the solution, run towards it.

I prayed to the LORD, and he answered me. He freed me from all my fears.

Psalm 34:4, NIV

Growth in the Garden

Note #43 Reflections

Note #44

The world is hard enough so do not beat yourself up. Be kind, gentle, and appreciate yourself because if you do not, who will?

Your kindness will reward you, but your cruelty will destroy you.

Proverbs 11:17, NLT

Note #44 Reflections

What things have you been beating yourself up about and why? What weight/significance do those things hold over you? How can you better appreciate yourself?

Taneka Lewis

Note #45

Do not fall for an illusion of what you think you need confusing it with what you want. It is a lie pretending to be the truth.

You live in the midst of deception; in their deceit they refuse to acknowledge me, declares the LORD.

Jeremiah 9:6, NIV

Refer back to your Note #33 Reflections

Note #45 Reflections

Taneka Lewis

Note #46

Do not give people positions they are unqualified for just because you are in an undesirable place. Stop allowing unqualified people to disqualify you. Not everyone will see your worth; do not let that person be you.

Your beauty should not come from outward adornment, such as elaborate hairstyles and the wearing of gold jewelry or fine clothes. Rather, it should be that of your inner self, the unfading beauty of a gentle and quiet spirit, which is of great worth in God's sight.

1 Peter 3:3-4, NIV

Note #46 Reflections

Taneka Lewis

Note #47

Heartache and pain are the hallway leading you towards an awakening. In everything you thought would end, you found new beginnings.

You were taught, with regard to your former way of life, to put off your old self, which is being corrupted by its deceitful desires; to be made new in the attitude of your minds; and to put on the new self, created to be like God in true righteousness and holiness.

Ephesians 4:22-24, NIV

Growth in the Garden

Note #47 Reflections

Note #48

Peace does not mean the absence of chaos. It is the calmness in the midst of disorder. Your peace can keep you from falling to pieces.

Now may the Lord of peace himself give you his peace at all times and in every situation. The Lord be with you all.

2 Thessalonians 3:16, NLT

Note #48 Reflections

Taneka Lewis

Note #49

Forgiveness...a beautiful pain where you have to put someone who did not meet your expectations before yourself yet forces you to look at your issues even more. Forgive so you have an opportunity to feel something else. How much is your hurt worth?

But when you are praying, first forgive anyone you are holding a grudge against, so that your Father in heaven will forgive your sins, too."

Mark 11:25, NLT

Growth in the Garden

Note #49 Reflections

Taneka Lewis

Note #50

You are strong. But is carrying the weight for everyone else how you want to exercise your strength? Lighten your load, let go of them and hold on to yourself. Everyone's battles are not yours to fight. What are you willing to let go to help you grow?

Therefore, since we are surrounded by such a great cloud of witnesses, let us throw off everything that hinders and the sin that so easily entangles. And let us run with perseverance the race marked out for us, fixing our eyes on Jesus, the pioneer and perfecter of faith. For the joy set before him he endured the cross, scorning its shame, and sat down at the right hand of the throne of God.

Hebrews 12:1-2, NIV

Note #50 Reflections

Note #51

Do not minimize your problems to maximize someone else's. Always make time for yourself. You cannot give to someone what you do not have for yourself.

"And don't be concerned about what to eat and what to drink. Don't worry about such things. These things dominate the thoughts of unbelievers all over the world, but your Father already knows your needs. Seek the Kingdom of God above all else, and he will give you everything you need.

Luke 12:29-31, NLT

Note #51 Reflections

Taneka Lewis

Note #52

When you feel yourself beginning to envy or idolize someone allow yourself to explore what in this person reflects an aspect of yourself that is begging to come out and be heard.

Seek his will in all you do, and he will show you which path to take. Don't be impressed with your own wisdom. Instead, fear the LORD and turn away from evil. Then you will have healing for your body and strength for your bones.

Proverbs 3:6-8, NLT

Note #52 Reflections

Taneka Lewis

Note #53

When you navigate through yourself you can take a trip anywhere through anything. Get lost on your journey, create your own map.

For I have stayed on God's paths; I have followed his ways and not turned aside.

Job 23:11, NLT

Note #53 Reflections

Note #54

Do not focus all your attention on the end goal. Maintain the balance between the acknowledgement of your progress and not settling for where you are. Appreciate and build on your small victories. Enjoy your journey.

> Do not despise these small beginnings, for the LORD rejoices to see the work begin,...
>
> Zechariah 4:10, NLT

Growth in the Garden

Note #54 Reflections

Taneka Lewis

Note #55

You miss the idea of what you thought you had. Everything is not meant to last forever. That time is over and it is ok, it was only meant to last for a season. There will be bigger and better things to come. Figure out what you miss and the reason(s) why so that you can begin to prepare for bigger and better things that are meant to be in your life.

A voice said, "Shout!" I asked, "What should I shout?" "Shout that people are like the grass. Their beauty fades as quickly as the flowers in a field. The grass withers and the flowers fade beneath the breath of the LORD. And so it is with people.

Isaiah 40:6-7, NLT

Growth in the Garden

Note #55 Reflections

Describe a situation that fell short of your expectations? What is it that you miss about that situation? What did you learn from it that will prepare you for what is to come?

Taneka Lewis

Note #56

Negativity is only negative if you perceive it to be that way. It is our nature to seek improvement and better ourselves. Bring *negative* things to the forefront of your life with the intention of improving it to make it better.

Jesus knew what they were thinking, so he asked them, "Why do you question this in your hearts? Is it easier to say 'Your sins are forgiven,' or 'Stand up and walk'?

Luke 5:22-23, NLT

Growth in the Garden

Note #56 Reflections

Taneka Lewis

Note #57

Joy and happiness live on the other side of pain and sorrow. When it rains, it pours…to give your garden twice the water it needs to grow. There is hope; what you are going through will not last forever, your breakthrough awaits.

Have I not commanded you? Be strong and courageous. Do not be afraid; do not be discouraged, for the LORD your God will be with you wherever you go."

Joshua 1:9, NIV

Note #57 Reflections

Taneka Lewis

Note #58

Tough times are a reminder of your motivation.
Maintain and sustain your motivation,
remember why you started.

Yet what we suffer now is nothing compared to the glory
he will reveal to us later.

Romans 8:18, NLT

Note #58 Reflections

Taneka Lewis

Note #59

Forward progression begins with taking a step back. Shift your perspective and take a look at the bigger picture.

Commit to the LORD whatever you do, and he will establish your plans.

Proverbs 16:3, NIV

Note #59 Reflections

Taneka Lewis

Note #60

Your mind will always believe everything you tell it. Feed it faith. Feed it truth. Feed it with love. You cannot hate yourself into a version of yourself you can love.

Love is patient and kind. Love is not jealous or boastful or proud or rude. It does not demand its own way. It is not irritable, and it keeps no record of being wronged. It does not rejoice about injustice but rejoices whenever the truth wins out. Love never gives up, never loses faith, is always hopeful, and endures through every circumstance.

1 Corinthians 13:4-7, NLT

Note #60 Reflections

Taneka Lewis

Note #61

Do not let expectations taint or distract you from the reality of a situation. Your expectations do not *guarantee* your desired outcome.

Faith shows the reality of what we hope for; it is the evidence of things we cannot see.

Hebrews 11:1, NLT

Note #61 Reflections

Taneka Lewis

Note #62

Practice gratitude. Start and end your day by writing down or saying three things you are thankful for no matter how small they are. Gratitude drives happiness.

I will give thanks to you, LORD, with all my heart; I will tell of all your wonderful deeds.

Psalm 9:1, NIV

Note #62 Reflections

Taneka Lewis

Note #63

Take the time to consider what you value and what is most important to you; evaluate whether you are living a life that reflects that.

The tongue has the power of life and death, and those who love it will eat its fruit.

Proverbs 18:21, NIV

Note #63 Reflections

Taneka Lewis

Note #64

Often times we feel lost when we do not distinguish who we are from what we do or what we have done. Establish the difference.

"Before I formed you in the womb I knew you, before you were born I set you apart;..."

Jeremiah 1:5, NIV

Growth in the Garden

Note #64 Reflections

Note #65

Do not try to fight your emotions out of fear of feeling and understanding them. They are there for a reason; embrace them and let them guide you to a truthful, logical decision about your circumstance or situation.

Don't act thoughtlessly, but understand what the Lord wants you to do.

Ephesians 5:17, NIV

Note #65 Reflections

Taneka Lewis

Note #66

You have a responsibility to be *ready* to receive your calling. You may not feel *ready*, but when you do something you are not *ready* for, you grow.

Then Jesus declared, "I am the bread of life. Whoever comes to me will never go hungry, and whoever believes in me will never be thirsty.

John 6:35, NIV

Note #66 Reflections

What have you been avoiding using the excuse, "I'm not ready" or "It is not the right time?" Why are you making excuses for something that you are destined to do or become?

Taneka Lewis

Affirmation #1

On this journey, I will commit to the art of consistency and obsession of tending to my garden and maximizing my personal growth and development. I will explore and evaluate the things I have manifested to live out my destiny.

Place your name in the affirmation (i.e. I, (insert name) will...) and for the next 33 days read this three times at least twice a day; once silently to yourself, once out loud, and once out loud while looking at yourself in the mirror.

Affirmation #2

I will not be afraid to affirm the truth, my truth.
I will discover, decide, and define my distinction.
I will dismiss things that discourage my distinction.
I will devote my distinction to make a difference in my life and the world.

Place your name in the affirmation (i.e. I, (insert name) will...) and for the next 33 days read this three times at least twice a day; once silently to yourself, once out loud, and once out loud while looking at yourself in the mirror.

Taneka Lewis

Affirmation #3

I am beautiful and great.
I am thankful and humbly grateful for everything that I have and everything that is coming to me.
I am not always right and when I am wrong I will use it as an opportunity to grow and continuously evolve into my greatness.
Every step I take will be taken with a purpose to constantly grow and nurture my garden.

Place your name in the affirmation (i.e. I, (insert name) will...) and for the next 33 days read this three times at least twice a day; once silently to yourself, once out loud, and once out loud while looking at yourself in the mirror.

Thank you for embarking on this journey of my self-growth and self-development. We are constantly evolving and going through new experiences. I hope I have sparked your self-curiosity and that you will re-read this book in each transition of your life as different notes will resonate with you and where you currently are on your journey. Start a journal as situations and questions come to mind while you are reading and reflecting on the growth you can achieve with each note.

Scan the *code* below to find out more about committing to continuous self-growth!